WHAT
SMART
CHURCHES
KNOW

Identity Press

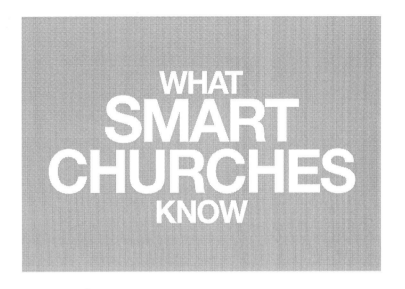

How Branding and Marketing Know-How Can
Revolutionize Your Church

ROD ARNOLD

Creator of the BrandSmart Method

Published in the United States by Identity Press,
an imprint of Q3 Marketing LLC.

ISBN 978-0-615-27908-4

Printed in the United States of America

www.BrandSmartMarketing.com

To Michelle, for 20 years of unconditional love.
May all your dreams come true.

Contents

SmartStep 4: STRATEGIZING

SmartStep 5: CREATIVITY

SmartStep 6: EXECUTING

SmartStep 7: OPTIMIZING

Who Needs This Book?

The process of writing this book has been quite a journey. When I began formulating the concept several years ago, the thought of putting these ideas into a written form for churches was exciting, and I launched into it with great enthusiasm. Then somewhere along the way doubts began to creep in. Not about the method or the ideas—I had seen them work without fail. It was more a sense of fear and trepidation. After all, this is the Church we're talking about—the Body of Christ. This is holy ground. Serious stuff. The last thing I wanted to do was treat the gospel like a product, because it clearly is not. Was I venturing onto dangerous ground? Honestly, it was a little scary to think about.

As I wrestled with this, I decided to go to scripture. I ended up in Matthew 25, the parable of the talents. Jesus tells the story of a master who was clearly pleased with the servant who invested money wisely.

But he was more than a little upset at the servant who did not even try to produce a positive return. Here's how the Message paraphrases the master's reaction in Matthew 25:26-30:

> *"The master was furious. 'That's a terrible way to live! It's criminal to live cautiously like that! If you knew I was after the best, why did you do less than the least? The least you could have done would have been to invest the sum with the bankers, where at least I would have gotten a little interest.*
>
> *"'Take the thousand and give it to the one who risked the most. And get rid of this "play-it-safe" who won't go out on a limb. Throw him out into utter darkness.'"*

Whoa, that's pretty strong! Apparently God's idea of stewardship is not just being careful with how much money we spend. He actually expects us to be smart and produce a positive return.

That's what this book is all about—stewardship. It's about churches using their time, talent and resources as intelligently as possible so they can achieve maximum productivity and reach more people. It's about being smart.

I am a big believer in the local church. I believe local churches are living, breathing communities God has designed for the purpose of helping, teaching and encouraging people. But sadly, I have seen so many churches actually do more harm than good with their marketing efforts. It grieves me to see churches waste their time—and God's money—when they really don't need to.

So I eventually came to the conclusion that not only was this book OK to do, but I *had* to do it. I don't want to run the risk of being a "play-it-safe" who gets thrown into utter darkness. I don't want to be one who commits the criminal act of living cautiously. By God's grace I have had some amazing experiences and learned invaluable lessons. This is information that churches need, and I am doing everything I can to be a good steward and get it into their hands. This book, my blog[1], my speaking engagements, my coaching services[2] — it all exists to help churches think and act smarter.

A Business Book For Churches

Let me be clear on what this is: This is a business book for churches. I have worked with local churches for many years, and one thing has become apparent: While the purpose of church is ministry, a church cannot thrive without following smart business principles and practices.

Whether you are a pastor, a church staff member, a lay leader or simply a concerned church member, you have probably noticed the disparity among churches and their ability to grow. While some churches see steady growth, others seem stuck at a certain size for years. What's the magic ingredient that makes some churches more successful from a numeric growth perspective?

The answer has nothing to do with magic. In fact, it most likely has little to do with the pastor's ability to teach or the quality of the music. It has been my experience that church growth is typically more impacted by issues of leadership and business expertise. But unfortunately, most seminaries and Bible colleges do a much better job of preparing pastors to preach and teach than to lead and manage. And that's why I believe this book is needed.

---

[1] www.BrandSmartChurch.com

[2] www.BrandSmartMarketing.com

This is not a comprehensive leadership and business management book; rather it's a how-to manual focused on several of the most important business concepts for churches: positioning, branding and marketing. It is my hope that you'll learn some valuable information and be inspired and motivated along the way.

But since this is a business-oriented book for churches, I realize it's not for everyone. In fact, here are a few questions to help you determine whether this book is for you:

1. Are you satisfied with the number of people your church is currently reaching?

2. Do you believe the people in your community have the correct and full perception of what your church really offers them?

3. Do you believe your church hits the mark on exhibiting excellence as a representative of Christ?

4. Are you satisfied with the results you are getting from past or current marketing efforts?

5. Are you satisfied with the "return on investment" for the dollars you are spending on church growth and/or marketing?

6. Are you easily offended by the use of business terms and concepts in the context of the local church?

7. Are you confident that you or someone on your team has a comprehensive understanding of branding and marketing best practices?

8. Are you opposed to learning new concepts and motivating others on your team to do the same?

If you answered "no" to more than a few of these questions, keep reading! This book is right for you, and I believe it will benefit you greatly. In the pages that follow, I will introduce you to the BrandSmart Method, a step-by-step guide to branding and marketing. I hope that as you implement these principles and strategies they will have a positive impact on your church. Please let me know if you have any questions, stories or ideas. I would love to hear from you!

Rod Arnold

Rod@BrandSmartMarketing.com

Web: www.BrandSmartMarketing.com

Blog: www.BrandSmartChurch.com

Introduction

Every day you are flooded with thousands of marketing messages. Think about how many messages came at you just this morning as you checked your email, visited your morning news websites, or turned on a morning TV talk show. Then they kept coming through the radio, on billboards, even on the sides of vehicles as you took your kids to school or drove to work. And that's just before 8AM!

The question is: How can your church make a lasting impression when your message is just one of five thousand a person will hear or see today? Especially when you're competing against Coke, Apple, Pizza Hut and all the other big dogs!

Well, don't despair if your church doesn't have millions—or even thousands—of dollars to spend on marketing. The good news is you don't have to be a "big dog" to get your message across. When you really break it down, marketing is simply communication, a discipline pastors and church leaders work with every week to influence people's minds. Do you want the people in your community to understand what your church is really all about? Do you want them to know how being a part of your church can benefit their lives? This book will help you do just that. You'll discover how to identify that special something that makes your church unique and appealing. You'll learn how to effectively communicate with the people in your city. And you'll understand how to make smart decisions about how you use your time, talent and resources.

Marketing is a discipline that is in flux; we are constantly seeing the introduction of creative ideas, innovative techniques and exciting new technologies. But the principles of marketing *strategy* remain unchanged over the years and decades. So while some of the practices presented in this book will eventually be outdated, the strategy and principles are solid and proven. You can take them to the bank.

The BrandSmart Method is a powerful model developed over many years of work, marketing a variety of churches, events, institutions, products and services. This book is loaded with proven principles, tools and practical tips—insights you don't usually get unless you've been in the trenches and seen what works and what doesn't. Along with the downloadable materials on my website, this book will help you approach positioning, branding and marketing intelligently, make the most of your church's limited budget and avoid common mistakes. Even if you have no marketing budget to speak of, following the steps in the BrandSmart Method can help you transform your church's presence in your city.

A New Age Of Marketing

Marketing has changed dramatically in recent years. People now rely on the Web as their primary source of information and help. They browse blogs, chat rooms and Web sites for answers. Many people are hurting or seeking, and they are looking for someone who speaks their language and addresses their unique needs. They are looking for rich, meaningful content, not just a slick design or catchy slogan. Your church is a potential source for all kinds of content that specifically addresses people's needs. You have what they are looking for. But is it available to them? Can they find it?

Do you want people to trust your church and look to you as a source of help? Do you want people to turn to you for answers again and again? Then you need to provide great online content. I'll show you how to intelligently and effectively use the Web to draw people to your church.

You Can Do This!

If you've visited your local mega-bookstore lately, you've probably seen the countless books chronicling huge marketing success stories. Companies like Google, Starbucks, Harley-Davidson and other heavy hitters.

If you've ready any of these books, you most likely felt inspired by their stories and intrigued by some new ideas. But can any of this really work for marketing a church? And how do you get from being inspired to actually experiencing some of this success for yourself?

Contrary to what you may have been led to believe, marketing is not a mystical art that only a few prodigies are able to master. Granted, the most successful companies are usually loaded with talented marketers and creative people, and it's easy to get star struck when you see what they've accomplished. But if you were given backstage access, you would find that the secret of their success is something much less glamorous: The common denominator among successful marketers is a best-practices approach that has helped propel these companies to superstar status.

The BrandSmart Method is a proven model—a master plan that works for businesses, and it works for churches as well. No matter your tradition, your style of worship, the size of your church, or the socio-economic makeup of your community, these are proven principles that absolutely work.

First Things First

To get started, let me give you a bit of a primer. Throughout this book I'll be using some terms that you've probably heard, but you may not have a clear understanding of what they really mean.

Prospect

In a business context, a *prospect* is a potential buyer of a product or service. For our purposes however, prospects are people in your city or town who could potentially attend your church. We'll discuss how to identify, profile and target prospects with the purpose of bringing them into your church.

Positioning

The objective of positioning is to find a window into people's minds. By discovering their needs and desires, and identifying that "special something" your church has to offer, you can help people make the connection between their needs and your church. Positioning defines who you are to people; it is the art and science of creating real meaning in people's minds about your church.

Branding

The objective of branding is to evoke an emotional response in people's hearts and minds. It includes creating key designs and messages that define your church "brand," but it goes beyond that to include every way in which people experience your church. What images come to mind when people think of your church? What emotions do they experience? Is it consistent with what you want them to feel? This is branding.

Marketing

Marketing, in particular *direct marketing*, is all about compelling the prospect to take a desired action. The objective of marketing is to elicit a specific response. For example, you may want people to visit your church, attend an outreach event, call a phone number, bring their kids to an event or donate to a capital campaign.

NOTE: Most people don't make the distinction between positioning, branding and marketing. They just talk about "marketing" as a whole. And actually, that's OK. Marketing should always start with positioning and branding. As I'll explain in the coming pages, marketing tactics do not work effectively unless you have first built that foundation. That's the purpose of the BrandSmart Method—to take a smart, strategic approach to marketing your church.

Common Mistakes

Unfortunately many people—including many professional marketers—don't have a comprehensive view of positioning, branding and marketing, and often they make some critical mistakes.

Mistake #1

The first mistake people make is that they perceive branding as a practice reserved only for elite companies or megachurches with multi-million dollar advertising budgets. This simply is not the case. As I'll explain, branding is equally important for all churches—large, medium and small. Even for those with little or no marketing budget. And thankfully, it does not have to be extremely expensive.

Mistake #2

Another common mistake people make is thinking of marketing as simply a set of tactics, such as direct mail, email, newspaper ads or radio spots. Unfortunately churches often fail to get the foundation of positioning and branding right, so those tactics are not as effective as they should be. If you go out and buy time on your local radio station to run ads, and you haven't gone through the foundational processes, there is a very good chance your marketing tactics won't get the results you expect and you'll end up wasting money.

Mistake #3

And finally, well-meaning people lack a consistent, proven approach to marketing their church. Marketing is not effective if you take a shotgun approach. That's what the BrandSmart Method is all about. This book will help you think strategically and get it right.

The BrandSmart Difference

What makes the BrandSmart Method different is that it is based on the belief that positioning, branding and marketing can—and should—work together to achieve maximum results. They are not isolated activities, and they should not be viewed that way. The smart approach is to identify your church's unique position, and then build a strong church brand by presenting messages to prospects in a way that reinforces your desired brand identity and compels people to respond.

And here's another important point. This method is not just something I came up with by brainstorming around a conference table and scribbling on a whiteboard. The BrandSmart Method works because it is based on proven principles and the best practices of successful companies, non-profit organizations and churches. It's a progressive process that will help you lay a strong foundation and then build on that foundation. This book gives you a master plan for marketing your church—the essential structure and tools to deliver results.

In the chapters that follow, we'll walk through the seven essential "SmartSteps" of the BrandSmart Method.

The BrandSmart Method

SmartStep 1: Positioning

[handwritten: How to express personality]

Learn to identify and articulate that special something that causes people to <u>feel a connection with your church.</u>

SmartStep 2: Branding

Discover the keys to expressing your church's personality and values through what people see, hear and experience and how it makes them feel.

SmartStep 3: Goal-Setting

Specifically define what you want to accomplish through marketing and learn how to measure success.

SmartStep 4: Strategizing

Become a master marketing strategist as you learn to identify opportunities, create detailed action plans and build budgets to meet your goals.

SmartStep 5: Creativity

Learn how to get the most out of creative people and the secrets to creating effective marketing designs and messages.

SmartStep 6: Executing

Understand how to turn your designs into actionable marketing materials and deliver them to your target audience with a punch.

SmartStep 7: Optimizing

Discover how testing, learning and adapting can help you get the most from your marketing efforts.

In each chapter, you will discover important principles and understand how to apply them. For some of the SmartSteps, I have included practical tools that I use when I coach church leaders. These are available for download on my website, www.BrandSmartMarketing.com. And along the way I'll also recommend additional resources that you may want to check out if you have an interest in going deeper on a given subject.

Are you ready to dive in? Let's get started!

SmartStep 1

Positioning

Positioning: Get Inside Their Heads

The first and most important step to intelligent branding and marketing is a concept called *positioning*. Positioning is foundational to the success of everything else you do in marketing. Even if you never send a direct mail piece, place a magazine ad or run a radio spot, positioning is critical and invaluable.

Strategy is King

When you talk to most people about marketing, they immediately think of the creative components—attention-grabbing concepts, cool slogans and slick designs. But more important than any design or tagline is *positioning*. Creativity is how you express yourself, but positioning defines who you are. Essentially, positioning is the process of identifying and articulating that special something that causes people to feel a connection with your church.

The objective of positioning is to articulate the unique promise you are making to people, with emphasis on "unique." In other words, what can you say about your church that no other church in your area can say?

Another way to think about this is...

- When people think about your church, what emotions and images come to their minds?

- What about people who have never been to your church? What do they think of you?

- What *unique* promise do you offer people? Is it really unique? Can any other church in your area legitimately make the same promise?

Here's an important concept to remember: It's not good enough to be better; you must be *different*. And not just different in *your* mind, but different in your *prospect's* mind.

Did you catch that? This is critically important! Positioning is about perception, because to the people you want to reach, perception is reality. You are intimately familiar with your church and it has significant meaning in your life. But unfortunately, for the purposes of marketing, *what you think doesn't matter*. The only thing that really counts is what is in the minds of your prospects, the people you want to reach.

Positioning is not something you do to your church—it is what you do to people's minds about your church. If you honestly believe that your church has something special and unique to offer people, positioning will help you communicate that special something to people in a way that really appeals to them and helps meet a need in their life.

There are two aspects of positioning that are important to understand: *position* and *positioning statement*.

Position

Begin Inside The Prospect's Mind

Your church's *position* is simply a depiction of how it is perceived by people—the place your church brand holds in their minds. That's why it's so important to begin by getting inside the mind of the prospect. A position is not something you tell people; rather it's what they tell you about your church. Focus on your prospect's perceptions, not your own. It's cold, hard reality, and sometimes it can be hard to swallow. But good leaders aren't afraid to define reality.

In fact, if budget allows, third-party research can be a great tool for helping you understand your current position. If that's not an option for you, people in your community who do not attend your church, or newer people in your church (not your core people, rather those on the fringe), can probably offer some pretty good feedback. However, honesty is key, and people don't like to deliver bad news...especially to the pastor. Consider having someone other than a pastor or church leader approach them and ask for their honest opinion, or conduct a blind survey. Ask what comes to mind when they think of your church. What one word or phrase would they use to describe your church? Boil down those answers to get the real answer to the question, "What position do we own?" It's important to know the truth, whether it feels good or not.

Seeker Personas *Individual Ministries Target Mkt.*

Once you really understand where you stand with people in your city or town, it's important to get a clearer picture of exactly who your prospects are, what makes them tick, and how your church can appeal to them.

In the business world, we create something called *buyer personas*, which are essentially snapshots of different types of potential buyers of a product or service. In the church context, we call them *seeker personas* to represent specific types of prospects we want to target. By developing a profile for each seeker persona, we can do our best to put ourselves in their shoes as we build our strategy and create content, messages and designs. We'll dive into seeker personas much deeper in the next chapter, but remember this: Great church marketing focuses on the seeker first.

Positioning Statement

A *positioning statement* is different than your position—it expresses how you *want* people to view your church. It's the goal, the place you want to hold in their mind—the "special something" you want people to associate with your church.

What position do you want to own? "Own" is the key word—don't waste your time and money if another church already owns it, or if it's too big of a stretch to get to from your current position. Ask yourself, "Can we get there from here?" For example, if your church is well-known in town as "traditional" and you want to own "edgy," the painful truth is that it's probably not going to happen. (Plus there's a good chance you'll end up looking cheesy if you try.) A better option would be to identify a position that's more closely associated with "traditional," such as "trustworthy" for example.

Another possibility is that your research may reveal that your church does not currently own a singular position. But that can be a good thing! It means you have an opportunity to identify an opening in the prospect's mind that fits with your church's DNA and build a branding strategy to own that position.

The process of truly understanding your current position and creating an aspirational[3] positioning statement is critical to the success of all your marketing efforts.

Your church's positioning statement should express the following:

- Who you are

- Who your prospects are

- The specific needs of your prospects

- Who you are co-laboring with (more about "co-laborers" coming up)

- What makes you different than those co-laborers

- What unique benefits a person derives from your church

Then the key is to simplify your positioning statement and boil it down to one clear, simple concept. This concept will be crucial as you develop your branding and marketing strategy going forward. We'll

---

[3] The term "aspirational" here means something you are shooting for, or aspiring to.

walk through the process of creating a positioning statement in Chapter 3.

Authenticity And Consistency

As you develop a positioning strategy and define the position you want your church to own, there is one critical factor to keep in mind: It must be *authentic*. Don't attempt to own a position that is not consistent with your church's DNA. If people feel misled or if you come across as disingenuous, you will quickly end up owning a different position—one that you won't like.

And for your positioning to really be successful, you must be consistent week after week, month after month, and year after year. Don't expect everyone to get it immediately, but if you are authentic and consistent, you will begin to see people's perception of your church align with your desired position.

2

Creating Seeker Personas

Smart marketing begins with the prospect in mind. The overwhelming tendency for marketers is to focus on what *they* think makes their product or service great, and to build their marketing campaigns from that perspective. The same thing happens with churches. Often pastors and church leaders have a vision from God for the church, and that vision becomes the foundation for their branding and marketing. Now please hear me on this—I am not discrediting the vision from God. But unless He gave you specific instructions for how to present that in a marketing campaign, the smart approach is to begin inside the mind of the people you are trying to reach.

For example, the slogan "Glorifying God in Central City" may work for your core church people, but it probably has very little meaning to people on the outside. So this may not be the best marketing approach to take.

Who Are Your Prospects?

The first question to ask yourself is, "Who do we want to reach?" Now, I know the temptation here is to say, "Everyone! We want to reach everyone!" And I agree—your heart's desire should be to reach everyone. But there is an old axiom in marketing that you should keep in mind: *if you target everyone, you'll appeal to no one.* Most companies cannot serve everyone—to succeed they must choose a segment to focus on—or *target.* And churches have the same dilemma. As much as you may want to reach everyone, you are much better served if you identify who your primary target is so you can focus your strategy and messaging.

Don't fall victim to the Everybody Syndrome. You can't be all things to all people, so it is important to narrow your focus. Even though you'll welcome anyone who walks through your doors with open arms, for the purposes of marketing, it is important to identify the specific types of the people you are most capable of reaching, or that you feel called to reach.

I challenge you to narrow your focus as much as possible. Think of the people in your community as a target. You want to reach all the people on the target, but for the purposes of marketing it's important to start with the bulls eye—those in the very center.

Who is your primary target? You may say "unchurched people." That's great, but who specifically are they? What characteristics make them unique? Are they young, blue collar families who live close to your church building? Are they older retirees? Are they immigrants living in an adjacent neighborhood? Are they college students from the nearby university? Take some time and think about your target, and prioritize which groups you want to focus on first.

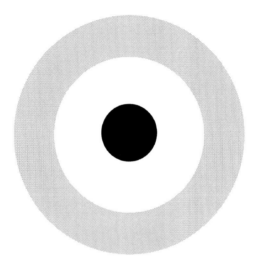

One thing I've noticed from working with churches is that the types of people they are most likely to reach are often represented in their church already. If the groups you have made a top priority are not already in your church, it can be more difficult to reach them. Just keep that in mind as you prioritize your target groups.

The Seeker Persona

Once you have identified the types of prospects you want to target, it can be helpful to create *seeker personas* for them. You've probably heard of the political equivalent of a seeker persona, such as Soccer Moms and Joe Six Pack. One famous example of identifying a seeker persona is Saddleback Church in California. In his book, *The Purpose Driven Church*[4], Rick Warren describes Saddleback Sam as the typical unchurched man who lives in his church's immediate area. By identifying a group of people with a moniker like Saddleback Sam, it makes it easier to keep marketing messages and content focused on the prospect, where it should be.

Who is the group you are targeting? Consider giving your seeker personas actual names to help them come to life. Maybe you'll end up with Northdale Norm, Kingston Karen or Johnstown Johnny. Have fun with it. But remember never to use these names publicly—they should be for internal use only.

The Seeker Persona Profile *Ea. Ministry to do:*

Remember, smart marketing begins with the prospect in mind. That's why it is critically important that we fully understand the needs and mindset of the people we are targeting. We need to get inside their heads and discover what makes them tick. By doing this we can create a *seeker persona profile* for each target group. You can download a free Seeker Persona Profile template from my website to make this easier, but essentially you want to answer the following questions about each seeker persona:

1. Are they in certain social or professional circles?

2. Are they in a certain income range?

3. Do they live in specific neighborhoods or areas of town?

4. Are they of a certain ethnicity?

---

4 Warren, Rick. *The Purpose-Driven Church*, Michigan: Zondervan, 1995.

5. Do they have a certain religious background?

6. Any other demographic specifics you can identify, such as age or family status? Are they single or married? Do they have children? Younger or older children?

7. What are their goals and aspirations?

8. What are their problems and pain points? (Not just in terms of church or faith, but life in general. Are they suffering financially? Are they worried about losing their jobs? Are they concerned about climbing the social or corporate ladder?)

9. What obstacles or struggles do they face on a daily basis?

10. What frustrates them?

11. Where do they go for answers to their problems? What media do they use?

12. What are common words and phrases they use?

13. What kinds of images and ideas would appeal to them?

14. What images and ideas would turn them off?

15. What else should we know about them?

One result of going through this exercise is that you may discover you don't know your prospect as well as you should. A great way to learn more about people is to spend time with them. Interview them. Listen to them. Subscribe to the media that they subscribe to. Go to the places they go to. It is important to put yourself in their shoes and truly understand what influences their decisions.

You should create seeker persona profiles for each target group you identified as an important priority. If you only have one, that's great. However, to help simplify and focus, I recommend beginning with no more than three.

You will refer back to the seeker persona profiles as you develop your positioning statement, brand identity, marketing strategy, messaging and designs. Digging into the mind of the prospect will help pave the way for success in all of your marketing efforts.

3

The Positioning
Discovery Exercise

One of the most powerful tools in the BrandSmart Method is the Positioning Discovery Exercise, which helps guide your team through an interactive discussion, culminating with a positioning statement that will serve as your guide as you develop your branding and marketing strategies. You can download a printable version the Positioning Discovery Exercise worksheet from our website.

One note before we get started. This exercise of developing a positioning statement is usually at least a half-day process and should involve key leaders in your church, including pastors, staff and lay leaders. It is best led by someone who is not closely involved in leading the church who can be objective and challenge your assumptions. I recommend locking your group in a room with some big flip charts, plenty of coffee, and going for it. OK, let's walk through the exercise.

Question #1: Who Is Your Prospect?

If you already went through the work of creating seeker persona profiles, this should be a no-brainer. Write down what you know about your prospect. Identify their specific characteristics—where they live, their income range, their religious background and their family status.

If you identified more than one seeker persona as priorities for your church, list information for the top three personas separately.

Question #2: What Are Your Prospect's Needs?

Again, you should already have this information on paper if you have created seeker persona profiles. List the specific needs of the people you are trying to reach: their pain points, struggles and frustrations.

One note on this: It is common for church leaders to immediately identify "Jesus" or "God" or "faith" as one of their prospect's primary needs. And obviously this is always true. But it is important for you to think in terms of *felt needs*. In other words, even though what they really need is a relationship with God, they may not feel that need on a daily basis. What they feel might be loneliness or stress. Think about it from their perspective, and try to identify what they are feeling.

Now, before you move on, I want you to go back through your list of felt needs, and identify four or five of the most prevalent needs. Put a star next to those.

Question #3: Who Are Your Co-Laborers?

If this were a normal marketing book geared toward the business community, I would dedicate this section to talking about competitors. But I know this can be a touchy subject because you are not in the business of competing directly with other churches. We are all part of One Church, and that's the attitude we should have. So I'll refer to other churches in your area as "co-laborers." The objective of this discussion is not to talk about how you can put the church down the street out of business–let's make sure we're clear on that. The real objective of positioning, branding and marketing your church should be to reach those people who are not currently being reached.

Let's face it, there is not a single church that can reach everyone in your community. It takes all kinds. But most unchurched people don't know the difference between one church and the next. The goal of positioning your church is to clearly articulate how your church is unique and how it can meet a need in their life.

So take some time to identify some of the prominent churches in your area, or at least categories or types of churches.

Question #4: What Are The Features Offered By Your Co-Laborers?

Once you have identified your co-laborers, now spend some time talking more about them. What are the *features* offered by each of them? Features are facts and objective characteristics that can be compared and contrasted. To get the juices flowing, take some time to discuss these questions for each of the co-laboring churches you identified:

- Is it in a convenient or central location?

- What's the size of the church?

- What's their style of worship and preaching/teaching?

- How many services do they have?

- How long are their services?

- How are they perceived in the community? Do people trust them? Do people have a favorable opinion of them?

- What programs do they have? (Children, youth, college, etc.)

- Do their various programs have positive or negative reputations?

- What is a typical member like?

Now, like you did before, go back through the list and identify the four or five features that are most uniquely associated with each church.

Question #5: What Unique Features Does Your Church Offer People?

Now go through the same process for your church. Focus mostly on those things that differentiate your church. What are the unique features that your church offers people? Ask all the same questions about your church...and be brutally honest! When you're done, go back through and identify the four or five features most uniquely associated with your church.

Question #6: What Unique Benefits Does Your Church Offer People?

Next is the most important step in this exercise. In the previous two steps we talked about *features*, characteristics that are relatively factual and/or quantifiable. Now we want to talk about *benefits*. Benefits refer to how your prospects' needs are met, either functionally, emotionally or in how they express themselves.

Benefits are derived from features, but the difference is that they speak directly to how the prospect's needs are met. For example, if one of the needs you identified in question #2 above was that "parents are worried that their teenagers will get involved in the wrong crowd," and one of your church's unique features that you identified in step 5 was "a strong, active youth ministry," a benefit might be that your church "supports parents by offering their teens a fun, worry-free environment and opportunities for positive friendships."

Benefits can usually be placed in one of three categories:

- *Emotional benefits* make people feel a certain way (e.g., happy, confident, satisfied, accepted, etc.).

- *Functional benefits* help people accomplish something more easily or effectively. (e.g., convenient location, lots of parking, three service times, etc.).

- *Self-expressive benefits* make people feel good about themselves by associating with a brand. For example, driving a luxury car projects success, or wearing a certain style of shoes projects coolness.

This will take some work, but spend time really digging into the unique benefits your church offers prospects to meet their needs. And again, once you've finished, go back through and identify the two or three most important and unique benefits on your list.

Your Positioning Statement

Once you've completed these steps, you should be ready to write your positioning statement. Here is an example of what a positioning statement might look like:

- *Who*: First Community Church

- *What*: is the local church in Mytown

- *For whom*: focused on 30-something, middle-class married couples with young children who live within a 15-mile radius of our church building,

- *What need*: who feel lonely and are looking for quality adult friendships.

- *Compared with whom*: Instead of traditional religious services and social status-oriented congregations that often leave them feeling disconnected and left out,

- *What's different*: we teach and encourage an authentic relationship with Jesus, and we embrace their family with genuine love in a cheerful, upbeat environment.

- *So that*: So they will enjoy coming to church, build meaningful relationships and feel a part of our community.

This is just a fictional example, but you get the idea. Keep in mind that your positioning statement should be unique to your church, and the more specific and focused you can be, the better. At this point this positioning statement is not for public consumption, and it still needs to be boiled down one singular position you want to own. In this example, First Community Church condensed their positioning concept down to "the cheerful, welcoming church," which addressed a legitimate need of their prospect, was consistent with their church culture and was not "owned" by any other church. They will design their brand identity around this concept, choosing colors and images to match. And this idea of "cheerful and welcoming" will be prevalent in their marketing designs, their messaging and the content they produce.

What position could your church own? Some other possible positions to consider include: family-oriented, interactive, progressive, young, trusted, community impact, powerful worship experience or possibly a certain theological position. The list is almost endless.

The Importance of Objectivity

As I mentioned earlier, the Positioning Discovery Exercise is normally at least a half-day process, often lasting an entire day. Bringing in an objective outsider to help lead this process can be very beneficial. Remember, positioning is the foundation of all branding and marketing. If you end up with a positioning statement that is not clearly defined, not truly unique, or not consistent with your church's culture, the entirety of your branding and marketing strategy will be on shaky ground.

If you would like some professional help in this process, I offer a one-day coaching option. If you would like more information, please don't hesitate to contact me.

Rod@BrandSmartMarketing.com

SmartStep **2**

Branding

4

Branding: Making Your Mark

Once you have gone through the process of positioning and identified a singular concept that you want to own in the prospect's mind, the next step is to create a *brand identity*. When we talk about brand identity, we're really talking about the tangible expression of your church's personality and values. It's what people see and hear—and how it makes them feel.

Why Does Brand Identity Matter?

People's awareness and recognition of companies, products, churches and other brands are facilitated by a visual identity that is easy to remember and easily recognizable. And that visual identity influences their perceptions and associations. The words they consistently read and hear impact their opinion. People automatically make judgments—about what your church is like, what your values are, and what kind of people you are—based largely on the brand identity you convey. In other words, whether we like it or not, people do judge books by their covers.

Getting your brand identity right is critical if you want people outside your church to know who you are and what you're about. It's also important to continually reinforce those ideas for people who are already a part of your church, in part so that they can easily articulate it to their friends and neighbors.

In fact, even if you have no marketing budget, having a clear and well-developed brand identity can, over time, have a significant effect on your church's position among the people in your city. As people see and hear the expression of your personality and values—and if it is authentic—their attitudes and opinions can begin to shift. And if you have gone about it the right way and addressed the real needs of your customers, the result should be more people interested in your church.

Brand Identity Essentials

Simplicity

Some of the strongest corporate brands are also some of the most simple. Think about how simple the marks and color schemes are for brands like Apple, Google, Coke and Hershey's. Avoid the temptation to create elaborate logo designs with lots of colors and graphics. It may seem cool to you, but that doesn't necessarily mean it's effective.

Authenticity

Before we jump into the specifics of how to develop the components of brand identity, it is important to keep things in context. You will waste a lot of time and money on branding and marketing if you miss one critical concept: *You must deliver on your promise.* We have all been disappointed or frustrated—or even angry—when we made a purchase, only to find out out the product or service did not live up to its billing.

If your branding and marketing promises people a certain experience or certain values, you must be able to live up to those expectations. The last thing you want is for people to be disappointed, because it is very likely that they will share their sentiments with others in your community. If they expect one thing and get another, they will perceive you as being dishonest. Not only is that bad business, God's probably not too keen on it either.

Consistency

One of the keys to successful branding over the long-term is consistency. If you are not consistent in how you express yourself, and you do not offer people a consistent experience, they will perceive you—whether consciously or subconsciously—as having a sort of multiple personality disorder.

Imagine if you knew someone who always dressed, talked and fixed their hair completely differently each time you saw them. You would be confused. What are they really like? What's their true personality? Well, the same is true with churches.

For example, many churches who have not established a clear brand identity send mixed signals. Sometimes they're serious and sometimes they're whimsical. Sometimes they seem intense, and other times they come across as light-hearted. Some communications look very formal, while others look very casual. Do your best to be consistent over the long term.

The Complete Brand Experience

Creating a brand identity is only one component of branding your church. It's important to consider all the ways in which people come into contact with your church. What do they experience when they visit your website, or pull into the parking lot, or walk into the lobby, or enter the sanctuary, or take their kids to the nursery? This is why it's important for your brand identity to be authentic and the brand experience to extend to all areas.

The interesting thing about your church is that it extends beyond the walls of your church building. A church is a community of people. The only experience many people have with your church is their interaction with members of your church at school functions, at work, at the store or talking with their neighbors. So how can you control the brand experience when it happens through touching other people? Well, unfortunately you can't *control* those types of experiences, but you can *influence* them. If your positioning and brand identity are authentic, it should make an impact on the people in your church. For example, if you are the "cheerful, welcoming church," that cheerful, welcoming spirit should wear off on your people, and it should show through when they interact with others.

And it doesn't hurt to reinforce your branding with your people either. If you have certain words or phrases that you want to be identified with your church, use those words and phrases consistently through all types of communication, including from the platform. The more they hear it, see it and experience it, the more likely they are to live it and communicate it to others.

Objectivity

I realize I have already mentioned this, but it is so easy for church leaders to become internally focused and, without even realizing it, make themselves irrelevant to those outside the church. Sure, you may like what you see, but does it communicate well with your prospect? Get some outside advice and feedback during the process of creating your brand identity.

5

A Quick Brand Audit

Before I go any further and explain how to develop your church's brand identity, step back for a moment and take an inventory of your church's current branding and how well it fits—or doesn't fit—the positioning statement you developed in Chapter 3. I'll take you through a quick brand audit, and you can also download the Brand Audit Worksheet from my website.

Brand Audit Questions

Logo

1. Do you have a church logo?
2. In what places and materials does your logo appear?
3. Do people outside your church recognize your logo and associate it with your church?
4. Do people in your church recognize your logo?
5. What do you think your logo communicates about your church?
6. Does your logo adequately represent your church's positioning concept to the people you want to reach?

Language

7. What tagline(s) does your church use?
8. What other phrases or vocabulary do you use in communications?
9. Do the words and phrases you use sound "churchy" or are they words and and phrases your prospect would use?
10. Do the words and phrases you use adequately represent your church's personality and positioning concept to the people you want to reach?

Typefaces

11. Are there a few typefaces you consistently use in communications, or do you use many different typefaces?

12. What style are the typefaces you use? (traditional, modern, plain, fancy, etc.)

13. What do you think your typefaces communicate about your church?

14. Do the typefaces you use adequately represent your church's personality to the people you want to reach?

Colors

15. What colors do you consistently use in church communications?

16. What do you think those colors communicate about your church?

17. Do the colors you use adequately represent your church's personality to the people you want to reach?

Images

18. What types of images do you use in your church communications?

19. What do you think those images communicate about your church?

20. Do the images you use adequately represent your church's personality and positioning concept to the people you want to reach?

General

21. Does the signage outside and inside your church building match your other colors, images, typefaces and language?

22. Are you consistent with the colors, images and typefaces you use across all communications? (including advertisements, signage, bulletins, video projection, website, etc.)

23. Do you have rules and standards in place to ensure consistent use of colors, images and typefaces?

Based on your answers to these questions, you probably have a pretty good idea whether you need to take a harder look at your church's brand identity. Thankfully there are some principles and guidelines to help you create a brand identity that truly represents your church's personality and positioning concept.

6

Creating Brand Identity

Creating a brand identity can be very expensive. In fact, it's not uncommon for large companies to spend hundreds of thousands of dollars on the process. But take heart—it does not have to be expensive for your church. Unless you have access to talented creative people with marketing experience, you will want to bring in outside help. But it does not have to cost you thousands and thousands of dollars.

Follow these steps to develop the key components of your brand identity.

Articulate Your Church's Personality

Think of your church's personality like you would an individual's personality. For starters, get together with the group you worked with on the Positioning Discovery Exercise and answer these questions together. What terms would describe your church? Is your church..

- intense or whimsical?
- solemn or joyful?
- formal or casual?
- structured or free-flowing?
- traditional or modern?
- older or younger?
- masculine or feminine?

Are there any other personality traits that describe your church?

Write Key Marketing Copy

Once you have articulated your church's personality, it's time to create what we call *key marketing copy*, which is text that can be revised for use in various marketing applications. For starters, take the positioning statement you came up with in SmartStep 1, and turn it into marketing copy. In other words, break it up and rewrite it into sentences and phrases that flow in a conversational way that connects with the casual reader. Unless creative writing is your strong suit, I strongly recommend working with a professional copywriter or someone in your church with a gift for writing.

Visit the Resources section of my website for some examples of key marketing copy.

Develop A Tagline

A tagline is a short phrase that captures your church's personality and positioning, and distinguishes your church from other churches. Taglines affect customer actions by evoking an emotional response. Even though they seem simple, a tagline should not be taken lightly. Done right, it is the most frequently used and strategically powerful expression of your church's positioning.

A good tagline has the following characteristics:

- short, optimally 2-5 words
- unique and distinct from competitors
- captures the brand personality and positioning
- easy to say and remember
- no negative connotations
- evokes an emotional response

Developing a tagline can be a long and involved process, typically because people have so many different ideas. This is another area where you may want to consider bringing in outside expertise to help.

Choose Colors

The next step is to work with a graphic artist to create the brand identity visual components. Keep in mind, there is a science to this. Color creates emotion, triggers memory and gives sensation. A good artist will work with you to identify a palette of colors that match your church's personality.

Keep in mind these basics when choosing colors:

*   According to most psychological studies, variations of red, orange and yellow (so-called warmer colors) are more effective at grabbing our attention. This doesn't mean all your colors should be attention-grabbing, but you should at least incorporate one or two secondary colors that are.

*   The ultimate goal is to "own" a color that people automatically associate with your brand.

*   Color is dramatically affected by various file formats and media. You must test repeatedly.

*   In corporate product marketing, estimates are that 60% of the decision to buy a product is based on color.

Ask the following questions when developing a color strategy:

*   Is the color distinctive?

*   Is the color differentiated from other churches?

*   What do you want the color to communicate?

*   Is the color trendy, or will it continue to work over time?

*   Does the color work on white?

*   Does the color work on black?

*   What secondary colors are possible?

*   Can you keep the color consistent across various media?

- Will this color work in signage?

- Have you developed both a web palette and a print palette?

Choose Typefaces

Choosing the right font for your church requires a basic knowledge of typeface options and an understanding of how typography can function effectively. Here are some basics for you to keep in mind:

- Typefaces are chosen for their legibility, their unique character and their range of weights and widths.

- The best brand identity guidelines identify a range of fonts but give users flexibility to choose the appropriate font, weight and size for the specific application.

When selecting typefaces, you try to find those that meet the following criteria:

- Convey feeling and reflect positioning

- Work for multiple application needs

- Work in a range of sizes

- Work in black and white, as well as color

- Differ from the other churches

- Are legible

- Have personality

- Are sustainable, rather than trendy

- Reflect the local culture of your community

Design Your Logo

Logos can be designed with an almost infinite variety of shapes and personalities. They can be literal or symbolic, word-driven or image-driven. Although there are no hard-and-fast rules to determine the best type of logo for your particular church, the designer you work with should explore a range of possibilities that serve your needs. Types of logos include:

Wordmarks

A wordmark is a distinct text-only typographic treatment. The church name is incorporated as a simple graphic treatment to create a clear, visually memorable identity. This can be one of the simplest and least expensive ways to express your brand. For example, think about how simple and recognizable some corporate wordmarks like are, like GAP, ebay and Google.

Letterforms

A letterform is a unique design using a stylized graphic treatment of one or more of the letters in your church name. An example from the corporate world would be CNN's letterform logo, which is an acronym for Cable News Network.

Emblems

An emblem is a logo design that includes your church name, as well as a pictorial element. YouTube and Domino's Pizza are two prominent examples of corporate emblems.

Pictorial Marks

A pictorial mark is a literal, recognizable image that has been simplified and stylized. Examples you would recognize include the CBS eye and the NBC peacock.

Abstract/Symbolic Marks

An abstract or symbolic mark conveys a big idea or an abstract design. A few of the most obvious examples are the Nike "swoosh" and the Mercedes three-pointed star.

Sub-Brands

Once the core brand identity is established, it's time to address your "sub-brands," the various programs and ministries of your church. This includes the youth ministry, children's ministry, outreach ministries, various adult ministries, and any other ministries of your church. Many churches have a dozen or more distinct sub-brands.

It's not a bad thing for each ministry in your church to have its own unique identity to an extent, but you should ask this question: Is the sub-brand consistent with the overall church brand direction? In other words, would someone on the outside know that this ministry is part of your church, and would it make sense to them? Does the sub-brand's personality fit with the church's?

What you'll find is that some sub-brands may need to be modified. And some may need to be cut altogether. This can be difficult because people get emotionally attached to these brands. But remember, building a brand can be expensive and difficult, so it's important to have as few brands as possible, and make sure sub-brands reinforce the master brand.

One way to address this issue is to create templates for communications like email blasts, web pages, bulletin inserts and video projection slides. Templates can give room for the individual ministry to exercise some creative liberty, but they provide consistency by placing the church's logo, tagline and some basic colors and/or images on everything that is published, tying it back to the church master brand.

Brand Identity Guidelines

The final result in this process should be a Brand Identity Guidelines document that your staff and ministry leaders can use to guide them in developing future communications. This document should give specific instructions for things like:

- logo usage

- sample marketing language

- color palette and where/how to use them

- specific images and types of images to use (including photos and graphics)

- acceptable typefaces and where to use them (for example, certain fonts for headlines, taglines, body copy, etc.)

The Brand Identity Guidelines document becomes a guide for everything that is created for public view, including things like:

- bulletins
- projection slides
- websites
- emails
- billboards
- newspaper ads
- TV commercials
- signage
- all other communication, whether it's to the congregation or to the general public

Additional Resources

For some examples of church Brand Identity Guidelines, visit my website. There you can also find help with copywriting and graphic design.

SmartStep 3

Goal-Setting

7

Marketing Goals: Know Where You're Going

We all know the importance of goal setting for success; it's hard to arrive at your destination if you don't know exactly where you're going. But if I were to ask you to identify your church's primary marketing goal, the answer may seem simple. "We want to grow!" Well, that's great, but you need to be much more specific in your goals so that: a) you can design the right marketing strategy, and b) you can know whether or not you are achieving success.

Objectives

When it comes to goal setting, it's important to start with your overall *objectives*. Do you want to...

- ✓ increase attendance?
- ✓ increase giving?
- ✓ position your church with a new image in the community?
- ✓ attract new kinds of people (e.g., younger families, professionals)?
- some other objective?

Do this right now. In the space below, take a few minutes to write down the top objectives for your church in order of priority.

Objective #1:

Objective #2:

Objective #3:

Marketing Goals

One you've identified your primary objectives, then ask yourself, "What specifically do we want to accomplish *through marketing*?"

SMART Goals

You're probably familiar with the SMART acronym related to goal setting, but it deserves repeating. Effective goals are:

S - Specific

M - Measurable

A - Attainable

R - Realistic

T - Timely

For example, if your objective is increased attendance, your SMART marketing goals might be:

1. Attract 40 new families to fall community outreach events.

2. Attract 50 new visitors over next three months to the singles ministry through the "bring a friend program."

3. Receive 100 new inquiries per month through advertising campaigns.

Note that these marketing goals are:

• Specific (families, singles, advertising-driven)

• Measurable (20 new families, 50 new singles, 100 new inquiries)

• Attainable (no astronomical numbers)

• Realistic (working through existing channels or networks)

- Timely (have timeframes attached)

Getting Started

When it comes to setting marketing goals, start with baby steps. You don't need to shoot for the moon right away. And don't necessarily set huge three- to five-year goals until you first set some short-term goals and discover what it takes to go out and achieve them. Remember, small victories will inspire people, lead to bigger dreams and help other people on your team believe in and support what you're doing.

One of the best ways to establish SMART marketing goals is to answer the following questions:

1. Who exactly is your target? (Make your goals specific to each seeker persona.)

2. What specific action do you want people to take? (Do you want them to call a number, visit a website, attend an event, or something else?)

3. How can you quantify your results to know if you're successful?

4. What is your goal in numeric terms?

5. By what date do you want to see results?

6. What channels, relationships or opportunities should you consider utilizing to help you reach your goal?

[handwritten note in left margin: Ch. ministry direction]

[handwritten note: Help to define vision, goals, achievements for each ministry objective]

Take some time to think through these questions for each of the objectives you identified earlier. You will come back to these goals as you build your marketing strategy and action plan in SmartStep 4.

8

Web Content as Marketing

Up to this point, I have discussed marketing from a traditional perspective—messages and materials created with the sole purpose of eliciting a response. But there is another aspect to marketing that deserves attention. People are actively searching the Web for answers to their problems, and you have an opportunity to give them the information they are looking for.

In his book, *The New Rules of Marketing and PR*[5], David Meerman Scott writes, "Great content brands an organization as a trusted resource and calls people to action—to buy, subscribe, apply, or donate. And great content means that interested people return again

---

[5] Scott, David Meerman. *The New Rules of Marketing and PR*, New Jersey: John Wiley & Sons, Inc., 2009.

and again. As a result, the organization succeeds, achieving goals such as adding revenue, building traffic, gaining donations, or generating sales leads." You should have marketing goals in place for creating rich content and making it accessible to your prospect.

Built-In Content

The odds are that your church is producing great content every week through sermons and Bible studies at a minimum. But how accessible is that content to the people who are not inside your four walls? Are you putting audio or video of your services on the Web? Do you podcast? Do your pastors have blogs? What about transcribing the talks into downloadable PDF's? Do you have chat rooms or discussion boards around the current sermon series? Do you have a Facebook group for your church? There are many ways to get your content out there for people. And if it's good content, those people will want more information, and some of them will eventually end up in your church.

Press Releases

In addition to publishing the content your church is creating, don't overlook the importance of having news coming out on a regular basis. Your church should have press releases going out to local media and online services for all kinds of things. Do a press release for an upcoming event or guest speaker, and then do another one after the event happens. Do a press release for the upcoming youth mission trip. Send another one while they're on the trip, and another when they return. Highlight interesting stories from your church members' lives. Send a press release when a church member achieves something significant. Find news on a weekly basis, get it out to the media and get it on your website.

I will discuss online marketing in upcoming chapters, but many of the details of how to build a content-rich Web presence are beyond the scope of this book. I highly recommend you pick up David Meerman Scott's book and take steps toward getting more of your church's content on the Web in as many formats as possible. Make Web content one of your objectives and set goals for reaching people online.

SmartStep 4

Strategizing

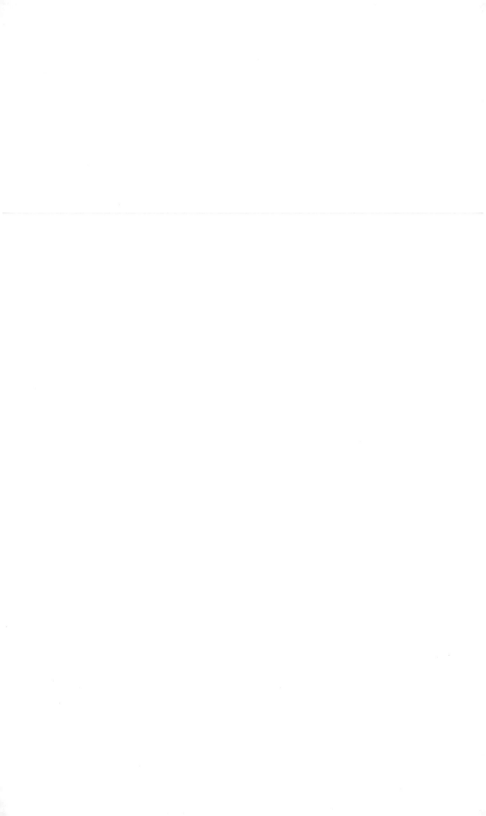

9

Marketing Strategy: Planning for Success

After you've gone through the process of determining your marketing goals, now it's time to design an action plan and a budget to meet those goals.

Determine Your Overall Budget

The first step is to determine how much money you have to work with to achieve the goals you've set. One note here: If marketing is a new venture for you, you don't need a million dollars (or even thousands) to get started. And a marketing plan does not need to be extensive at the beginning. You can even just start with a few tests if you like. Don't be afraid to get your feet wet before diving into the deep end.

Sample Marketing Plan

I highly recommend you go now and download the sample marketing plan from my website. As you will see, I have put together a fictional marketing plan and budget, which I'll refer to throughout this chapter. I'll walk you through creating the plan, referring to fictional people as we go.

Back in Chapter 8 I listed several sample marketing goals. This is a plan for the achieving the first goal I listed: *Attract 40 new families to fall community outreach events*. And we have a total budget of $4,000. Each goal you set should have its own specific marketing plan and budget.

Marketing Plan for: First Community Church

Goal 1: Attract 40 new families through fall outreach events
Total Budget: $4,000

Assets And Opportunities

I always start a marketing plan by identifying what assets and opportunities are available for me to leverage. In this example, we have two events planned for the fall, a Labor Day lake party and a Harvest Festival. We can also put current church members to work for us. Plus let's assume we have a good relationship with the local radio station.

Marketing Plan for: **First Community Church**

Goal 1: Attract 40 new families through fall outreach events
Total Budget: $4,000

Assets & Opportunities to Leverage:
1) Labor Day lake party
2) Halloween alternative Harvest Festival
3) Church members
4) Relationship with local radio station

Strategy 1

The next step is to break down the plan into individual strategies. The first strategy is to leverage the Labor Day lake party.

Tactic 1

There are two tactics we have identified to get our prospects to the lake party. First, we're going to create an invitation for church members to give to their friends and neighbors. Note that each marketing initiative should have both an *offer* and a *call to action*. This is critical. You must always think, "What's in it for them?" and "What action do I want them to take?" These are very important questions to answer.

In this case, the offer we're going to make is "free food, fun and games for your family." And our call to action is "RSVP by August 25th to reserve your spot."

Now, you can see that we're going to produce 1,000 invitations for church members to distribute, and we're projecting a 2% response rate, for a total of 20 RSVP's. And we have a budget of $500 to pull off this tactic.

Strategy 1: Leverage Labor Day lake party
Tactic 1: Invitation for church members to give friends & neighbors
Target Audience: Friends of church members
Offer: Free food, fun and games for your family
Call to action: RSVP by August 25 to reserve your spot
Goal: 20 RSVP's by deadline
Response Rate: 2%
Quantity: 1000 invitations
Budget: $500

Action Plan And Budget

So let's put together an action plan and budget for this tactic. Since the event is the first week of September, we need to work backward from there.

The first thing we need is to have someone write copy for the invitation. Now is the time to pull on those creative people in our church. Jacob is a good writer and is willing to volunteer his time to do this. (Plus he has gone through SmartStep 5 and learned the 10 rules for writing marketing copy.) So no cost there. And we're going to set July 15th as the deadline to have copy written.

Next we're going to have Jennifer design the invitation by August 1st, and she's willing to do that for us for $100. What a bargain. She'll get the copy from Jacob and finish the design by August 1st.

So that gives us two weeks to take Jennifer's design and have it printed by August 15th. Bill is going to oversee the printing process for us, and the printer is charging $400 to print the 1,000 invitations. Then finally, we'll distribute the invitations to church members on Sunday, August 25th. Suzy will make sure ushers are ready to hand them out and that there is plan for announcing and motivating church members to get involved.

That uses up our total budget of $500. And if we assume a 2% RSVP response rate on the 1,000 invitations and a 50% no-show rate, that should give us a total result of 10 new families attending the lake party. Pretty straight forward, right?

Timeline: Action	Target Date	Owner	Cost
Write copy for invitation	July 15	Jacob	$0
Design invitation	August 1	Jennifer	$100
Print invitations	August 15	Bill	$400
Distribute to members	August 25	Suzy	$0
		TOTAL	$500

Comments: Assume 50% no-show rate. Total projected result = 10 families.

Tactic 2

Now, as you can see we have another tactic that's also associated with the first strategy of leveraging the Labor Day lake party. Because we have a good relationship with the local radio station, we're going to allocate a good chunk of our budget, $1,500, to radio spots.

So again, we have the same offer and call to action. And our goal is to get 40 RSVP's from these radio spots. So we're going to run a total of 20 spots, and we're projecting a response rate of two RSVP's per spot that we run.

For this tactic, Jim is our guy. He's going to handle the entire project, including having the spot written, negotiating the purchase, and making sure the campaign launches on time. We're assuming a 50% no-show rate, so if we get 40 RSVP's from the radio spots, we're projecting that will result in 20 families actually attending.

Tactic 2: Radio spot campaign
Target Audience: Families not involved in a church
Offer: Free food, fun and games
Call to action: RSVP by August 25 to reserve your spot
Goal: 40 RSVP's by deadline
Response Rate: 2 per spot
Quantity: 20 spots
Budget: $1,500
Timeline:

Action	Target Date	Owner	Cost
Write and produce spot	August 1	Jim	$250
Purchase radio spots	August 1	Jim	$1,250
Launch campaign	August 25	Jim	$0
		TOTAL	$1,500

Comments: Assume 50% no-show rate. Total projected result = 20 families.

Strategy 2

OK, so that covers the lake party. But we also have the Harvest festival. Remember our goal was 40 new families attending fall outreach events. We're projecting our first strategy will yield 30 new families, so we're only ten short. However, since this is our first time using these strategies and tactics, we really aren't sure if our assumptions are right. So we're going to use our full budget and do everything possible to make sure we don't fall short of our goal.

So we have basically replicated the tactics from strategy 1 and applied them to strategy 2. However, keep in mind that we will have the results from strategy 1 before we move forward with strategy 2.

So depending on how well our tactics worked for the lake party, we may want to adjust our plans for the Harvest Festival.

Strategy 2: Harvest Festival
    Tactic 1: Create invitation for church members to give friends and neighbors
    Target Audience: Friends of church members
    Offer: Free food, fun and games
    Call to action: RSVP by October 20 to reserve your spot
    Goal: 20 RSVP's by deadline
    Response Rate: 2%
    Quantity: 1000 invitations
    Budget: $500

Timeline: Action	Target Date	Owner	Cost
Write copy for invitation	September 1	Jacob	$0
Design invitation	September 15	Jennifer	$100
Print invitations	October 1	Bill	$400
Distribute to members	October 10	Suzy	$0
		TOTAL	$500

Comments: Assume 50% no-show rate. Total projected result = 10 families.

    Tactic 2: Radio spot campaign
    Target Audience: Families not involved in a church
    Offer: Free food, fun and games
    Call to action: RSVP by October 20 to reserve your spot
    Goal: 40 RSVP's by deadline
    Response Rate: 2 per spot
    Quantity: 20 spots
    Budget: $1,500

Timeline: Action	Target Date	Owner	Cost
Write and produce spot	September 15	Jim	$250
Purchase radio spots	September 15	Jim	$1,250
Launch campaign	October 1	Jim	$0
		TOTAL	$1,500

Comments: Assume 50% no-show rate. Total projected result = 20 families.

This should give you a good idea of how to structure a marketing plan and budget, and the kinds of things you should be thinking about.

A Strategy for Web Content

As I explained in Chapter 8, getting your content on the Web is a great way to establish your church as a trusted resource and drive traffic to your site. Since church content is so much about issues and topics people are dealing with every day, accessing Web content will help people build an affinity and a connection with your church.

Just as you build a strategy and a plan for more traditional marketing efforts, you should also have a plan for your Web content. I recommend creating a Web publishing plan similar to the marketing plan above, with timelines, owners and budgets.

SmartStep **5**

Creativity

10

Writing with a Purpose

There are really two types of writing that I will address in this section—writing for *marketing* and writing for *content*. But regardless of the specific application, there are some principles that you should always keep in mind.

Watch Your Words

What your prospect really cares about is the benefit to them—how your church solves a specific problem in their life. And remember, they probably don't speak church language. There's a good chance that many of the words you're used to using have very little meaning to them. Don't use religious-sounding words unless you're targeting religious people. The words and phrases you use should be words and phrases the *prospect* normally uses.

This can be especially difficult for many church leaders, because they spend so much of their time studying scripture, reading theological materials and talking with other pastors and church leaders. I want to challenge you to spend more time out with the people you are trying to reach. Listen to them, and take note of the words they use in everyday conversation. When you really get inside the mind of your prospect, you'll be able to speak their language.

This principle applies not only to marketing materials, but to all the content your church produces, whether it's written or spoken. Who knows, you might even start to change the way you deliver sermons—and that might be a good thing. Here's a good rule of thumb: If you can substitute your marketing language for that of another church, then it's going to be very difficult for the prospect to understand why your church is right for them. Remember, it's not enough to be good, you have to be *different*. Use language that makes your church stand out.

When you sit down to create content or write a marketing piece, imagine yourself sitting in your prospect's home, having a cup of coffee at the kitchen table. Use words that have real meaning to them.

Words Impact Online Search Results

Another advantage of using the prospect's own words when you write is that it can positively influence online search results. Search engines like Google are more likely to find your website, blog or other online content if you use words people are naturally searching for.

Making Your Message Stick

In their best-selling book *Made to Stick*[6], Chip and Dan Heath outline the six qualities of ideas that stick in our minds. Incorporating these qualities into your writing is a great way to get the maximum impact from the content and marketing messages you create.

Simple

Boil your message down to its one core concept, and express it with as few, simple words as possible.

Unexpected

The best way to get people's attention is to break a pattern and surprise them. Then keep their attention by playing on their curiosity.

Concrete

Abstract concepts are easy to forget. Use concrete examples to help your prospect remember your message.

Credible

Why should anyone believe what you have to say? Use details, credentials, statistics and "internal credibility" to convince your audience.

---

[6] Heath, Chip, and Dan Heath. *Made to Stick*, New York: Random House, 2007.

Emotional

Experiences tied to strong emotions are much more memorable. Use the power of emotion to make your message stick.

Stories

Stories are powerful because they provide context—they make information more connected to our real lives.

I highly recommend the Heaths' book to anyone whose job involves communication, especially when you are dealing with issues of life, family and faith. One thing you'll notice is that this is the way Jesus communicated. Read their book, incorporate the ideas, and it will have a positive impact not only on your marketing, but on your sermons, books, blogs and every other type of communication you and your church produce.

Rules for Writing Marketing Copy

When writing for an advertisement, mailer or other relatively short marketing application, there are some tried and true rules to help you write as effectively as possible.

10 Rules for Writing Marketing Copy

Rule #1: Less Is More

For most marketing or advertising applications, less copy is best. Keep it clean. Think about how much time you give the average billboard—about a half second. Just one glance. You should think of other media the same way, such as newspaper or magazine ads, flyers, bulletin inserts or video projection slides. Don't try to say too much—just say one thing. Focus on your core message, the one promise that will resonate with the reader.

Rule #2: Focus On "You," Not "We"

Make the message about the customer. Say "you get," not "we give." It's a subtle change in approach that can make a world of difference.

Rule #3: What's In It For Them?

Remember, people don't care what you're doing, they're interested in how it will benefit them. You must translate features into benefits. Make it your goal to solve a problem for them. For example, "positive friendships and biblical training for your kids" is stronger than "children's programs for all ages." And "be refreshed and encouraged" appeals more directly to people's self-interest than "contemporary worship with biblical teaching."

Rule #4: Be True To Yourself

The marketing copy you write should consistently reflect your brand identity. The language you use should reflect your church's style and personality, whether it's traditional, modern, young, diverse —whatever fits your brand.

Rule #5: It's Only Funny Sometimes

Humor can be tricky, so use it wisely. With humor you run the danger of coming across cheesy, or of some people not getting the joke. Again, make sure it fits your brand identity. And keep in mind, humor typically hurts direct response rates. Use it with extreme caution.

Rule #6: Keep It Simple

Use short words. Use short, easy-to-read sentences. Enough said.

Rule #7: Hide It Under A Bushel? No!

The offer is critical. It's a statement of what's in it for the customer. Don't hide the offer or bury it in copy. State the offer boldly. And keep in mind, "FREE" is the strongest word in marketing.

Rule #8: Don't Save The Best For Last

Remember, most people will only read the headline, so make it count. Surprise endings are great for novels, but this is marketing. Put the most powerful stuff up front.

Rule #9: Remember Who You're Talking To

Narrow your audience and focus on them. Are you speaking to families with young children? Single mothers? Retirees? Who is your primary customer? Try to picture that person in your head. Remember, if you target everyone, you'll appeal to no one.

Rule #10: Focus On The Fundamentals

Every direct response marketing message should contain three essential ingredients:

- The offer: What's in it for them
- The call to action: What should they do and when should they do it
- How to respond: Give them email, phone number, website, etc.

Those are ten rules to live by when writing marketing copy. So now let's talk about design.

12

Rules for Marketing Design

Artists love to use their creativity to produce magnificent works of art. The only problem is that they don't always have an understanding of how to design for effective marketing. Help artists learn to use their creativity within these guidelines.

10 Rules for Marketing Design

Rule #1: Make It Easy To Read

This is probably the most challenging concept for graphic artists to deal with. Artists tend to go over the top on design, which can make the piece hard to read. What they are designing for you is not an artistic masterpiece; it has a singular purpose. Remember, the design must work for your marketing purpose, even if you offend an artist.

Rule #2: Make The Offer Stand Out

We covered this in the rules for writing copy, but it goes for design too. The offer is key, so make sure the design draws the reader's attention to it.

Rule #3: Don't Bury The Call To Action

Remember, people don't know what to do, so you have to tell them. The designer should make sure the call to action is easy to find.

Rule #4: Keep Design Consistent With Brand Identity

You went through the arduous process of developing a brand identity for a reason. Avoid multiple personality disorder and continue to build your church's brand. By being consistent with your design elements, you are subconsciously saying to people that you know exactly what you're doing and you can be trusted.

Rule #5: Avoid Reverse Body Copy

"Reverse copy" means light-colored type on a dark background. This is always more difficult to read and comprehend, especially when it's used in the body of a paragraph. Avoid it whenever possible.

Rule #6: Use Easy-to-Read Typestyles

The typeface you use should not draw attention to itself. The less fancy the better, especially on body copy or small fonts. Be sure to keep this principle in mind as you're developing your brand identity in SmartStep 2.

Rule #7: No Justified Or Condensed Type

Copy blocks do not need to fit a perfect shape. Don't squeeze or stretch a line of type. Remember, readability is key.

Rule #8: Don't Wrap Copy Around Shapes

We are accustomed to reading from left to right, from the beginning of the line to the end. Don't make people hunt for the next line.

Rule #9: Avoid Skinny Columns

Again, this is not how we're accustomed to reading. Make sure the columns of copy are wide enough for easy reading.

Rule #10: Use Colors That Grab Attention

According to most psychological studies, variations of red, orange and yellow (so-called warmer colors) are more effective at grabbing our attention. Again, keep this in mind when selecting the palette of colors for your brand identity in SmartStep 2. This doesn't mean all your colors should be attention-grabbing, but you should at least incorporate one or two secondary colors that are.

Rules for Specific Applications

Of course every media and every project are a little different. Here are a few pointers that for creating some specific applications:

Direct Mail

When thinking about direct mail I recommend you consider the 3 D's:

Differentiation

What's your message? How are you going to make your message jump out of the mailbox and demand attention? Be sure to consider unique paper types, colors, designs, and sizes. (Paper types and styles should be considered before you begin since they will affect the design.) If your budget allows, I recommend the use of oversized or die-cuts mailers that will help your message rise to the top.

Design

Take a moment and think about the mail you have received over the past few weeks. What pieces do you remember the most? Most likely they all included unique design, unique copy, or some other sort of "wiz-bang" that made the piece stand out. Don't get stuck in a direct mail rut—be creative with your designs. Although creativity can be limitless, its important that you work with your printer and mail house[7] to confirm that your design meets standard mailing regulations. Failure to meet postal specifications can significantly increase your postage costs or result in your mail piece being rejected by the post office.

Delivery

Be sure to discuss your delivery method with your designer, printer and mail house. Are you planning to send your mailing via bulk, first class, or special delivery? Each delivery option requires

---

[7] A mail house is a company that specializes in processing and sending direct mail.

specific design rules and regulations that must be met. Remember, start with the end in mind.

Print Media

When we refer to print media, we're talking about newspapers, magazines, newsletters and even bulletin inserts. You usually have less space available to you than in a brochure or direct mail piece, so it's important to be concise and direct. Let the audience be your guide; design with them in mind. For example, if you are designing an ad for a women's magazine, you'll approach it differently than an ad going in the sports section of the newspaper.

Television

On TV, you don't have many words available to you, so it's important to have strong visuals. Production value is very important. If you come across badly on TV, it can often do more damage to your brand than it does good. So a general rule of thumb is to not do it unless you can do it right.

Radio

Since it is so hard to squeeze information into a 30-second radio spot, I recommend going with 60-second spots. Start the spot on a positive note—don't turn people off. Try to fit the website or call to action in the first 15 seconds; it doesn't have to be a hard sell, just something that points to the website. Be sure to repeat the call to action several times at the end. And unless you have experienced, qualified people and equipment in your church, it's worth your money to have your radio spots professionally produced.

Email

Because people are inundated with email on a daily basis, it's important to keep yours simple and clean. Use a compelling subject line that captures their attention but doesn't feel like a gimmick. Focus on what's "above the fold," or the few inches of space that shows up in most email applications' preview pane. Be sure to capture email addresses of people who respond to offers. And design your emails with a combination of HTML and text to avoid getting caught in spam filters.

SmartStep 6

Executing

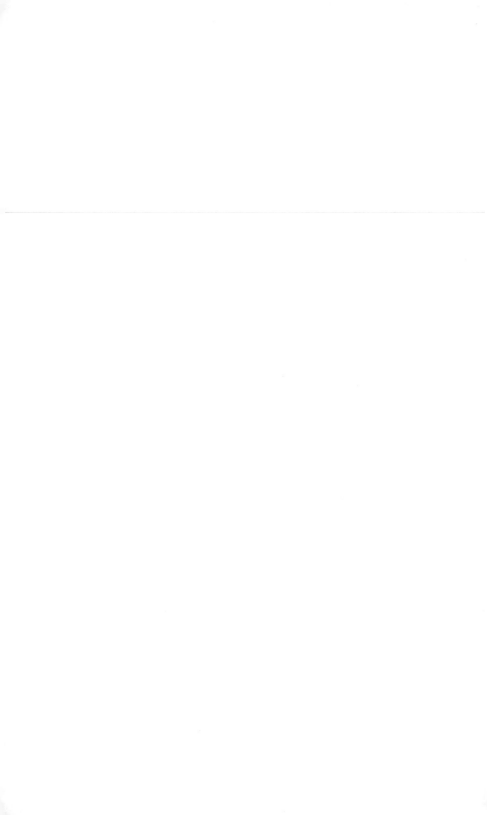

14

Direct Marketing

You've prepared, you've planned, and now you're finally ready to execute your plan and start seeing results. When we talk about marketing execution, there are really two components to consider: production and fulfillment.

Production

Production is the process of turning designs and copy into actionable marketing materials or properties. This includes things like printing a brochure, coding a web page or producing a radio spot.

Fulfillment

Fulfillment is the process of delivering the marketing materials or properties to the target audience. This includes US mail and email delivery engines, as examples.

For the purpose of execution, we can break marketing tactics into three categories: direct marketing, electronic advertising and traditional media.

Two of the most common forms of direct marketing, especially for churches, are direct mail and email. Let's start with direct mail.

Direct Mail

List Acquisition

As you've gone through the process of building your marketing strategy, you have determined a target audience for each campaign. The question then becomes how to reach that audience. For example, let's say that you want to send a direct mail piece to every house in a certain part of town. How would you go about doing that? This is where list rental[8] comes into play. You may be surprised to learn how much information is available to you. Database lists of potential customers are available and can be broken down by zip code, city, even specific neighborhood.

The way this normally works is that you "rent" a list for specific campaign, and pay a one-time use fee. Now, if those people respond to your campaign and you capture their address and other

---

[8] List rental is the rental of data for one time use. This can apply to mailing use where name and address details are supplied, or to telemarketing use where a partial address and telephone number may be supplied.

information, you now "own" that record and you can mail to them as often as you like without having to pay another rental fee.

The most common way to rent a list is to work through a list broker[9]. There are also some online services, some of which can be helpful. For references on list brokers and online services, please visit our website, www.BrandSmartMarketing.com.

Your goal should be to build a database of *records* that continually grows over time. A record includes a name, address and other personal and demographic information.

Printing Your Direct Mail Piece

Once you have your list and you know how many pieces you're going to mail, you are ready to meet with your print broker[10] or directly with a printer to choose the type of paper and the method of printing. There are many variations of paper to consider, including size, shape, thickness and the type of finish. You can also apply different types of varnish to the paper if you want certain elements to "pop," or really stand out.

Depending on the size of your mailing, there are three printing options:

---

[9] A list broker is an individual or company who negotiates the use of an owner's list by another individual or organization. A broker may also provide research, recommendation and evaluation services.

[10] A print broker is an individual who helps guide your printing decisions, negotiates with printers and acts as a liaison with printers throughout the printing process.

Digital Printers

Digital printers can be used for short-run mailers (2,500 pieces max). Printing digitally can be a bit limiting in terms of design, but also has some advantages. Usually you will get a quick turnaround and have the ability to personalize your mail piece.

Sheet-Fed Printers

Sheet-fed printers are the most common printers and typically handle mid-size print jobs (2,500 – 75,000 pieces). Sheet-fed printers are very flexible with design and often offer a large assortment of post-printing processes (i.e., binding, insertion[11], poly-bagging[12], etc.). Many sheet-fed printers also act as mail houses and are able to prep and deliver your final product directly to the post office.

Web Printers

Web printers[13] should be used for large print jobs (75,000+ pieces). Web printers are a little less flexible than sheet-fed printers but can often offer a much lower price on larger print jobs. Web printers almost always have mail services in-house and can prep and deliver your final product to the post office.

---

[11] Insertion refers to including a promotional item, such as a response card, inside a printed piece.

[12] Poly-bagging involves inserting a printed piece in a plastic bag, which also allows you to include samples of other materials.

[13] A web press is fed by paper from a reel as opposed to separate sheets.

Print Brokers

Since there are so many options available when it comes to printing, it can definitely be confusing. You may want to consider working with a print broker. Print brokers act as a liaison on your behalf to the print shops. They are able to bid your job to several printers and help you negotiate the lowest possible price without sacrificing quality or service. Visit my website for a list of print brokers I personally recommend.

You will usually want to have your graphic artist interact directly with the printer to deliver the artwork in the exact format they require. Once the art files are delivered, printers will produce a proof for you to review and approve before they go to press. Most printers will send you the proof in an electronic PDF format, which is quick and easy to review. However, keep in mind that colors always appear differently on your computer screen than they do on paper. What looks red in a PDF may end up looking pink or orange on paper. So I recommend requesting a hard copy proof from the printer before you approve it.

Delivering Your Direct Mail Piece

Once your piece is printed and ready to go out the door, it's important that you understand your options related to postage. Bulk and non-profit rates are usually available for churches, depending on the quantity, and can sometimes save you hundreds or thousand of dollars in postage. But keep in mind that bulk rate mailing requires some very specific ways of designing and bundling your pieces. If you're not familiar with these rules, consult your local post office.

Mail Houses

An easier and often more cost-effective way to handle bulk rate and non-profit mailing requirements is to work with a "lettershop" or "mail house." These are companies that specialize in fulfillment of mail and they are very aware of postal regulations. They also use specialized equipment, which can dramatically speed up the time it takes you to stuff envelopes, apply addresses, apply postage, sort and send. And often the cost of using a mail house is minimal, especially compared to the time and manpower it can take you to coordinate and/or manually complete the entire process.

For recommended mail house contacts, visit my website, www.BrandSmartMarketing.com.

Email

List Acquisition

The process for producing and fulfilling an email campaign involves steps similar to direct mail. For starters, just as there are lists available to rent for direct mail, there are also email lists available. However, this can be a tricky proposition. Many records in email lists are incomplete or lacking detailed locating information. For example, a record may include the state, or maybe even the zip code, that corresponds to the email address, but often they will not have any geographic information more detailed than that, such as neighborhood or exact address.

Another option is to work with local agencies or companies that have email lists of people in your city. A good example might be your local newspaper. Often privacy policies will prevent them from selling or renting their list to you, but if not, this can be a good option. One way to get around this is to place an ad in their electronic newsletter, if they have one. If you capture the information of the people who respond to that ad, those records are yours to keep.

Designing And Coding Your Email

While you're preparing your email list options, you can work on designing and coding the actual email. If you want to send a colorful, designed email, the best option currently for avoiding spam filters is to use a combination of text and HTML. You'll need to work with a designer and an HTML coder to prepare your email.

Sending Your Email

Once your list and your email are ready to go, the best way to send it out is to use an online email engine. Good email engines have built-in compatibility with large Internet service providers, such as AOL, Gmail and Yahoo, to avoid getting bounced by their filters. They also come with built-in tracking tools, so you can get a report on the number of bounces, opens and click-throughs.

15

Electronic Advertising

Web Advertising

One form of electronic advertising is to place an ad on a website. There are several options for placing your Web ad:

Direct To Web Sites

You can contact owners of specific websites directly and pay for an ad on their site. Depending on how sophisticated they are, you'll either pay a fee based on a daily, weekly or monthly rate; or they may charge you based on the number of *impressions*. By impressions, we're talking about the number of times your ad loads in someone's

Web browser. Neither of these are great options, because you can never be certain whether someone is actually seeing your ad. Even with impression-based pricing, it's possible that your ad could load "below the fold," which means it is outside the browser window and only visible if the person scrolls down the page.

Digital Ad Agencies

Another way to approach web advertising is to work with a digital advertising agency. These agencies can help you find the best websites to host your ad to reach your prospect. Some agencies have the technology to be very specific on which people see your ad, which can help optimize your budget. A drawback of this approach is that many agencies only work with companies with large advertising budgets. So depending on your budget, this may not make the most sense for your church.

Online Ad Placement Services

The third and usually the most practical way to advertise on the web is to use an online service. With online services like Adbrite, you can choose specific criteria for who sees your ad, and the service will place your ad on a variety of websites and blogs. And the good news is that you normally only pay for clicks, rather than impressions, which means you only pay for legitimately interested customers.

There are other online services that can be powerful vehicles as well. For example, Facebook can be a great option for churches, because you can choose very specific criteria for who sees your ad. Since Facebook users enter their address into their profile, you can narrow down your target customer based on geographic location, interests, groups they've joined and other criteria. And again, you normally only pay per click, rather than impression.

Paid Search

Paid search is a relatively easy and cost-effective way to advertise online as well. Services like Google Adwords allow you to set keywords and a monthly budget, and you bid on a per-click rate. If you do a search on Google, you'll normally see the *organic* search results on the main part of the page, as well as *sponsored* results either at the very top of the page and/or the right margin. When you use paid search, your ad will appear on the right side of the page, and where it appears is dependent upon how much you bid compared with other advertisers who selected the same keyword criteria for their ad.

Google Adwords has an online tutorial that makes this service relatively easy to use. For example, if your church is in Denver, your initial keywords might be "church" and "Denver." If your per-click bid is high enough, your ad will show up on the right side of the window. And Google Adwords will help recommend other keywords for you to add, based on the actual search patterns of people who also searched for "church" and "Denver." This can be a great tool and is relatively easy to use once you get into it and learn the system.

Search Engine Optimization

One of the most powerful methods of online advertising is also the most difficult. With search engine optimization (or SEO), the goal is for your church to show up as high as possible on the organic search results in online search engines like Google and Yahoo. SEO can be complicated, but if you have some budget money to work with, it can be money well-spent to hire an agency to help you.

16

Traditional Media

Designing ads for traditional media, including magazines, newspapers or newsletters, is relatively straight forward. These publications should provide you with specifications for your ad, including size, colors and bleed requirements. Usually your artist will upload your design to the publication's FTP site, and often they will send you a PDF proof to review, as well as a *tear sheet*, which is an actual sample of what was printed.

When purchasing space in print media, the general rule is to either go big or go small. If you can't afford a full page, drop down to a ¼ or ⅛ page. You'll usually get a better response for the amount of money spent. And generally the more color the better, so go with four-color over two-color or black-and-white.

SmartStep 7

Optimizing

17

Testing, Learning and Adapting

Once you have begun to execute your plan, the key to a successful ongoing marketing effort is to continually monitor and optimize results. Testing is just the smart thing to do. It's a matter of stewardship—to get the best possible result from your time and investment. Just because you like a marketing piece or it seems to work doesn't mean it couldn't work even better.

My testing model is simple:

Test → Learn → Adapt → Test again

It means that you are continually learning and looking for ways to produce better results.

What to Test

Test The Audience

The first variable to test is the audience. If you are focusing your efforts on various target prospect segments, you should measure how well each group responds to your offer. For example, you can measure results between different zip codes or neighborhoods. Or you can run offers aimed at different demographics, such as women vs. men, older vs. younger, or single vs. married.

A good way to segment and test your audience is through online search criteria, using services like Facebook that I explained in SmartStep 6. You can also monitor the results of ads in publications focusing on certain demographics. How does your cost per response compare between various target audiences?

Test The Offer

One of the primary drivers of response, of course, is the offer. I always recommend testing at least two versions of an offer whenever possible. For example, if you are doing an email campaign, most of your list might receive an offer of a free CD, while a smaller portion of your list gets an offer of a free booklet. We'll talk more about segmenting the list and testing methods in a moment. The idea is to always use what you believe is your best offer for the majority of your list, but also test a secondary offer and compare results.

Test The Copy

You can test different styles of copy, like a strong, straightforward appeal versus a softer approach. Or if your marketing piece includes a story, test different stories.

Test The Creative

Try testing different photos, different colors and different layouts.

Test The Format

For example, you can test a 4x6 postcard versus and oversized postcard versus a letter in an envelope.

Keys to Testing

For a test to yield legitimate results, it must follow several rules:

Make It Fair

Keep everything consistent except for the one key variable you are testing. You can't accurately measure results if you have multiple variables between test groups. For example, you can test the offer or you can test the creative, but you can't test both with the same group.

Make It Random

Be sure there is no bias based on who is tested in each group. For example, don't test one format with women and another format with men. Make the test groups completely random to get accurate results.

Measure Results Versus Cost

If you test two different formats and one is more expensive than the other, the best way to measure effectiveness is the cost per response, not pure response rate. After all, your goal is to be the best steward of your financial resources by getting the best results for your investment.

Advanced Testing Techniques

There are some advanced testing techniques for serious direct marketers that are beyond the scope of this material. If you are interested in concepts like regression analysis and response curves, I encourage you to check out the Direct Marketing Association[14].

---

[14] www.the-dma.org

Epilogue:

Becoming a Smart Church

What a tremendous privilege it is to serve in a local church. There are people all over the world who do not even have the right to worship freely. We have been blessed. And with that blessing comes responsibility. It's time for churches to be truly wise stewards of their time, talent and resources. It's time for churches to reach their God-given potential. It's time for churches to get smart.

Keys to Success

Whether you are a pastor, church staff member, lay leader or active volunteer, there are several keys that will help make the BrandSmart Method successful in your church.

Don't Short-Circuit The System

The BrandSmart Method is a comprehensive process, with each SmartStep building upon the previous. If you just take bits and pieces instead of going through the entire process, you won't get the results you're after. Commit to the entire method, and you'll be glad you did.

Be Consistent And Stay The Course

Church staff and lay leaders are notoriously busy, so it's easy to slip back into old habits and not stick with the plan. If you take the time and energy to develop your brand identity and build your marketing plans, don't throw away all that effort. Your faithfulness will be rewarded.

Be Realistic

Don't try to take over your entire city in the first month. Set SMART, short-term goals. Test your way in to a full-blown marketing plan. Achieve some small victories first, and then keep dreaming and planning bigger.

Get Buy-In From The Entire Team

It's great to assign someone as the point person for marketing, but they will quickly be frustrated if they do not have the support of the pastoral leadership and cooperation from the leaders of the various ministry areas. For this reason, many churches find it helpful to bring in an outside expert to give the vision and initiate the process.

Design Management Systems To Help Sustain The Branding And Marketing Model

If you develop brand identity guidelines, create templates and develop marketing plans, make sure you have the systems in place for people throughout the organization to easily use and implement the plan.

Final Words

Finally, just a few more things I want you to keep in mind as you go forward.

Trust God from the bottom of your heart;
don't try to figure out everything on your own.

Listen for God's voice in everything you do, everywhere you go;
he's the one who will keep you on track.

Proverbs 3:5-6 (The Message)

God is on your side. He wants His church to grow and reach as many people as possible. Ask Him for wisdom and guidance as you plan. Seek to represent Him with excellence in everything you do. Trust in Him, and I believe He will bless your efforts and help you achieve your goals.

Remember, you can do this! Marketing is not rocket science. It will take some work to get things up and running, but others are doing it, and so can you!

And keep in mind that my team and I are here to help. Remember to check my website, BrandSmartMarketing.com for free resources and recommendations. And subscribe to my blog at www.BrandSmartChurch.com for a regular flow of inspiring ideas and practical tips.

May God bless you richly and cause His Church to thrive!

About the Author

Rod Arnold empowers leaders and organizations to think smarter about strategy, brand building and marketing. For more than 15 years, Rod Arnold has trained and equipped church leaders to expand and improve their ministries. Through his agency, BrandSmart, and senior positions he has held at Integrity Music, Group Publishing and Teen Mania Ministries, Rod has been responsible for marketing and building such brands as Hillsong United, Integrity Live, Acquire the Fire, Dare2Share and Group. His years of work have led to the development of the BrandSmart Method, an innovative seven-step process for branding and marketing. Rod lives in Fort Collins, Colorado, with the love of his life, Michelle, and their four incredible children—Ben, Bo, Jackson and Lily.

Contact Rod to speak at your event or work with your team on strategy, branding and marketing.

Rod@BrandSmartMarketing.com
Web: www.BrandSmartMarketing.com
Blog: www.BrandSmartChurch.com